nature abhorring a vacuum

# A Pig's Ear
## Nonsense from the Pigsty

pig's tie

DRAWINGS AND VERSES
BY SIMON DREW

Antique Collectors' Club

to Caroline
and to Niki
(who have no
particular connection with pigs)
thanks to Philip Burley and to Sandi.

ain't nothing but a
bound hog

© 1994 Simon Drew
World copyright reserved

ISBN 1 85149 208 9

British Library Cataloguing in Publication Data
A catalogue record for this book is available from the British Library

Printed in England by the Antique Collectors' Club Ltd.,Woodbridge, Suffolk IP12 1DS
on Consort Royal Satin paper from Donside Mills, Aberdeen

the truth about the road hog

however hard you hunt,
if pigs are in the front....
I'll bet you a fiver
there's a back sheep driver.

I spy with my little eye
something beginning with 'O'

don't know

one pig

# A SHORT HISTORY OF THE PIG

The pig has been an important animal in human civilisation. This is probably because of its striking resemblance to humans: it is often pink, has a soft covering of hair, suffers from sunburn, has an omnivorous diet and, apparently, tastes much the same as human flesh.

It has taken part in many ancient fables and myths such as those handed down by the Greeks:

Leda and the Swine

Since biblical times the pig has featured in many parables and this has resulted in modern day proverbs:

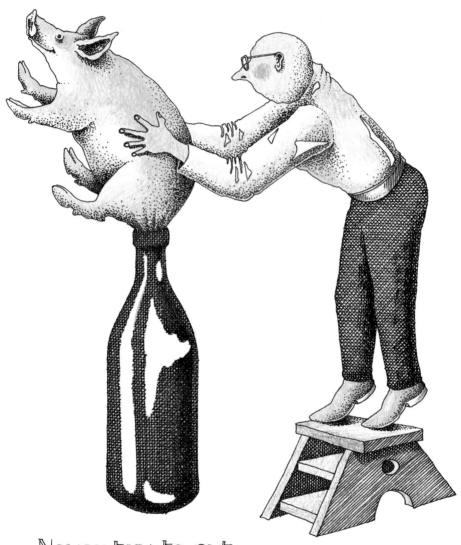

Never try to put new swine into old bottles.

More recently some people have wanted to remain anonymous so earnestly that they have even used porcine features as a disguise:

an unknown frenchman making a pig of himself.

Stories have often been told about talking dogs but a few years ago reports came out of Portugal of a remarkable piglet that accompanied a sardine fisherman when he played the piano.

large male with pair of wife runts

this little piggy went to Margate.

# A PIG'S TALE

what do we want ?

procrastination

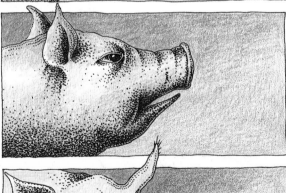

when do we want it ?

next week

# THE PIGS DILEMMA

When some people ask what I do.....
I try to recall what I've done.

The next line will rhyme with line two
and that line has rhymed with line one.

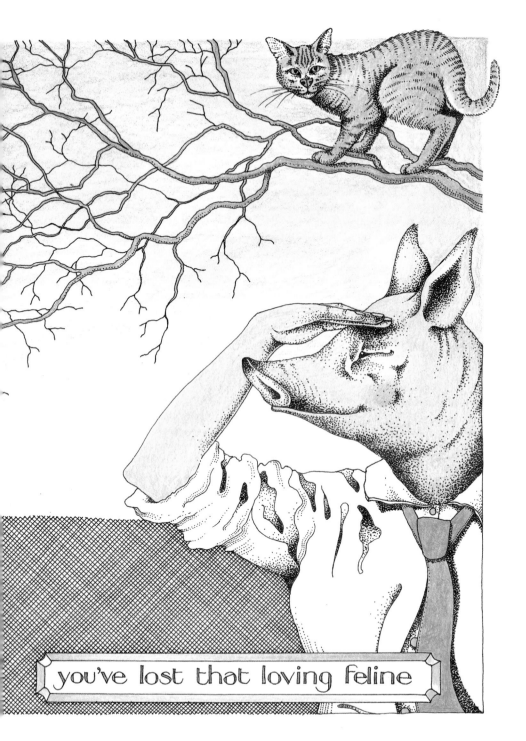

you've lost that loving feline

15

UNITED COLOURS OF BENIDORM

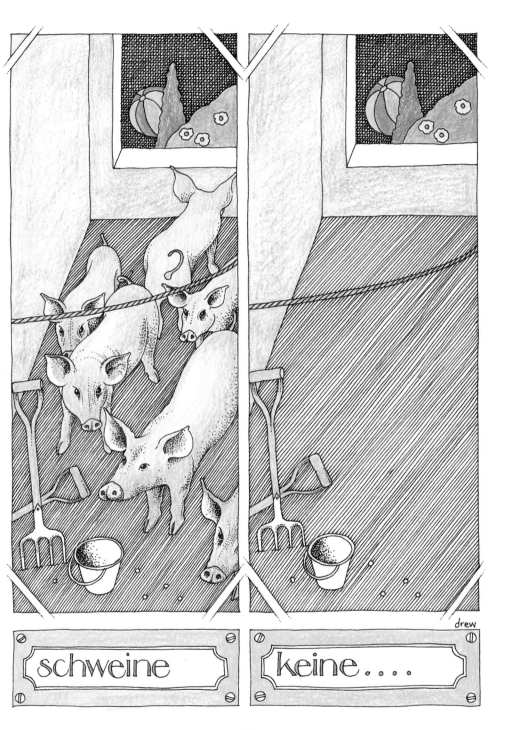

schweine

keine....

drew

17

# Great Surrealist Literature:

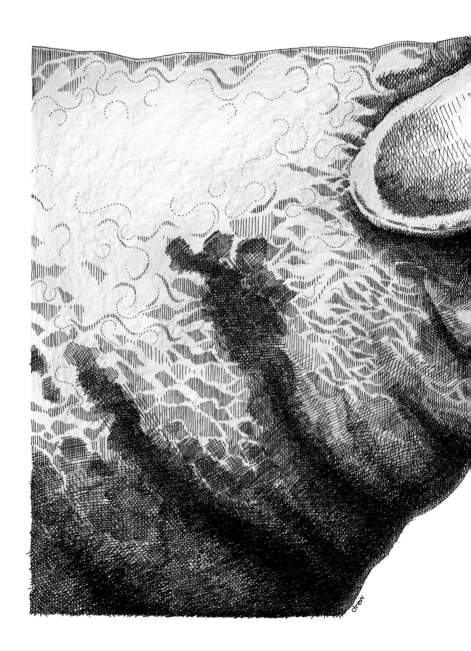

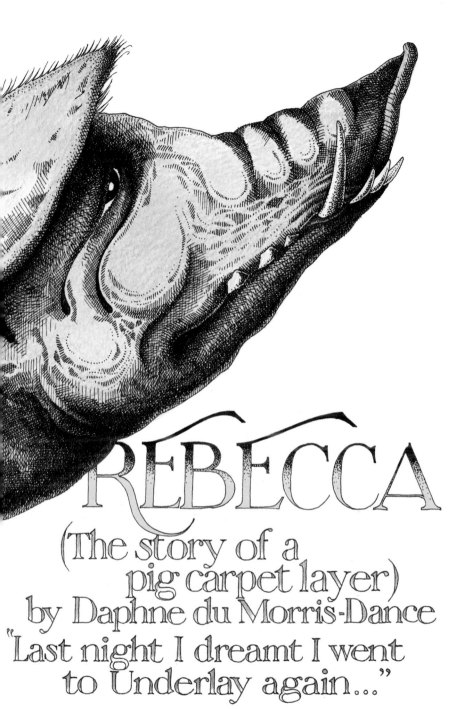

# REBECCA

(The story of a
     pig carpet layer)
by Daphne du Morris-Dance
"Last night I dreamt I went
     to Underlay again..."

# jehovah's waitress

..... seven swine a-swimming

A SQUARE PIG....

24

Blessed are the Pigmakers

# the carpenters

pig with a
hammerhead

bear with
a saw head

sheep worrying

I spy with my little eye something beginning with M

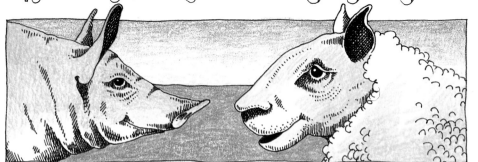

don't know

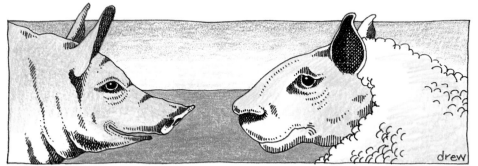

mint sauce

# vegetating vertebrates

a languid
lizard

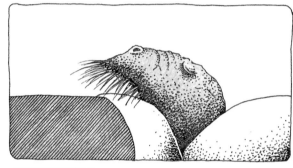

an inanimate
manatee

a supine
porcupine

a stationary
dromedary

a dormant
cormorant

a hibernating
viper (waiting)

a couchant
cochon

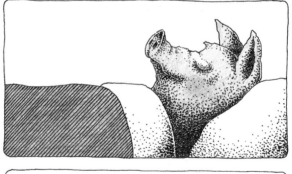

a railway
sleeper

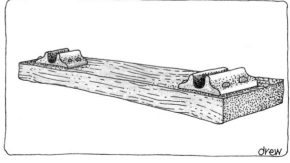

drew

a short story
in five
parts

# THE HUNTER

**1.**

I once met a pig in a sweat in a sauna,
  a shy and a secretive beast;
he lives in a house called hide-pork corner
  "somewhere" he said "to the east."
(He uses the sauna to keep himself pink
for pigs are more vain than a person
                    might think.)

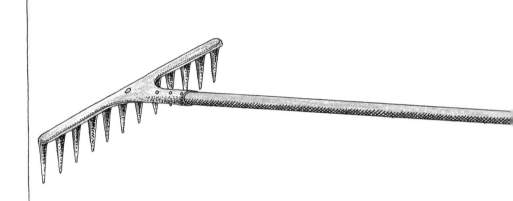

## 2

Life's pack of cards has been given a shuffle
   and dealt him a curious hand:
he has an ambition to hunt a great truffle,
   the greatest they'll find in the land.
He has no desire to seek second best;
this, he decrees, is the ultimate test.

drew

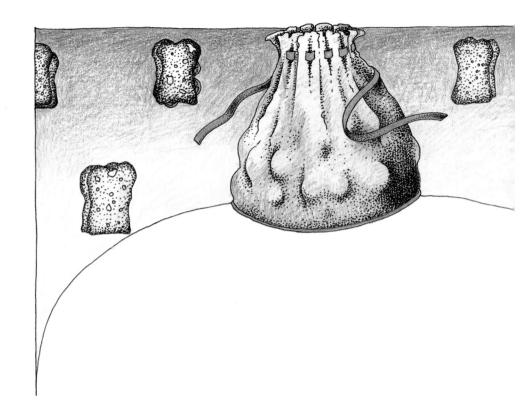

# 3

On Sundays he goes on his weekly
adventure,
his sandwiches bursting with cheese
(for though this gives trouble with bits in
his denture
the smell drives away all his fleas).
He carries a bag in a secretive way,
a bag that is heavy and canvas and grey.

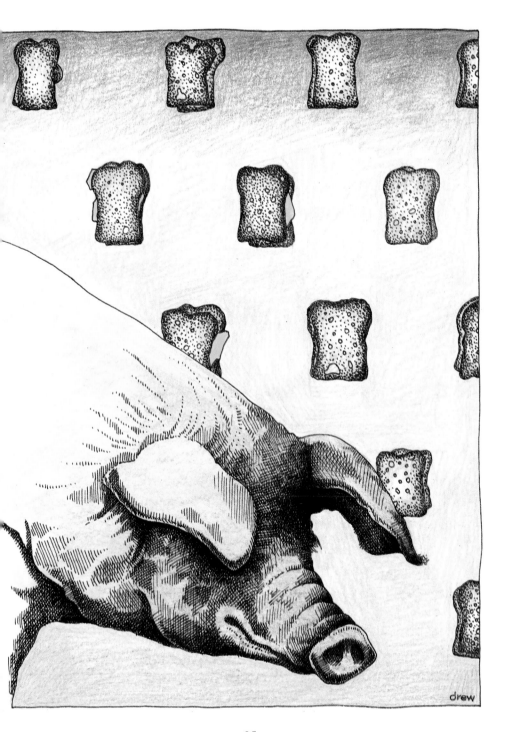

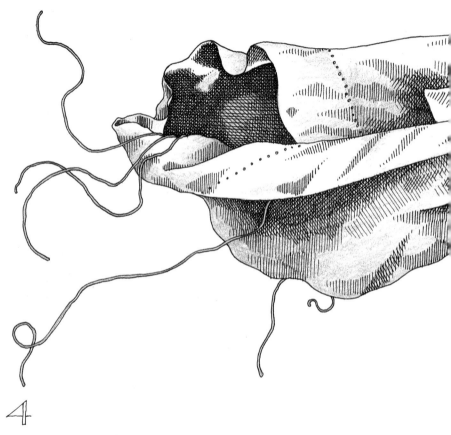

4

His nose is so large it's a problem to
measure
"That organ's immense", you'll declare.
It picks up the scent of the underground
treasure
with hardly a trace in the air.
This special proboscis is kept at its best
by keeping it wrapped in a light woollen ves

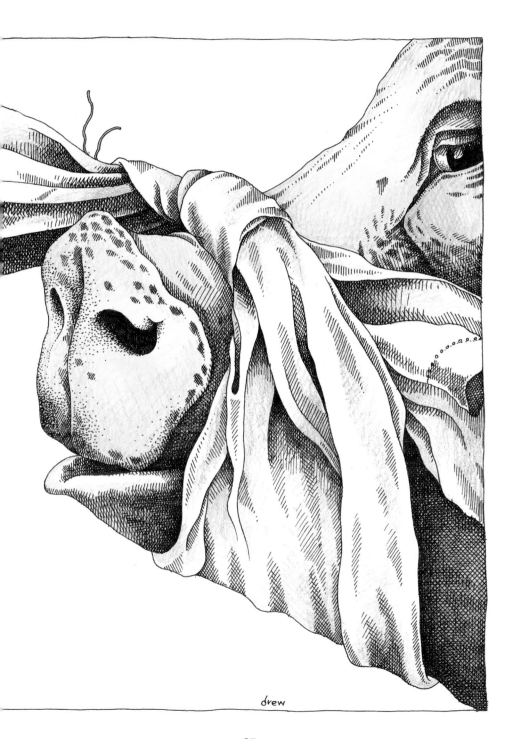

drew

## 5

And when he's made sure of a truffle's
location
He marks out the spot with some chalk;
This fine fungal growth is a dish's foundation
(although he can't eat it with pork).
He uses a shovel to dig a great pit
and calls it a tool in his best earther kit.

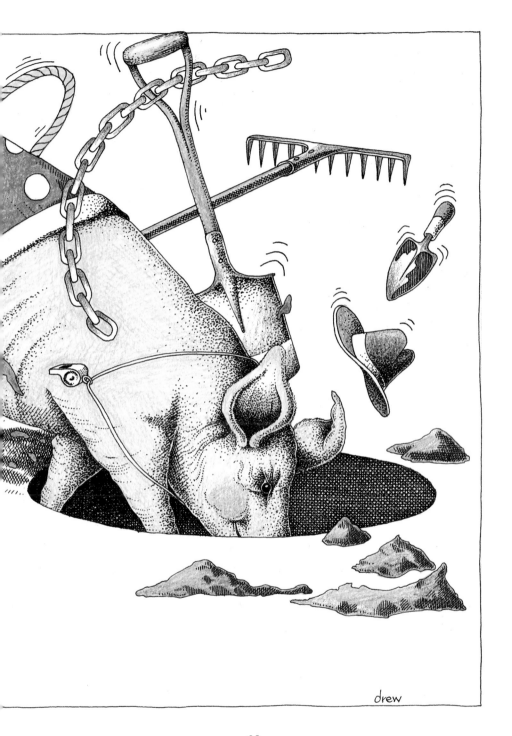

drew

"Wayne"

The moon was full as the Messerschmidt soared
and Kevin played with his parachute cord
Tracey was taking her pilot's test
and Wayne flew over the cuckoo's nest.

MEAT AND 2 REG

aside of bacon

# Great Discoveries of Biology

drew

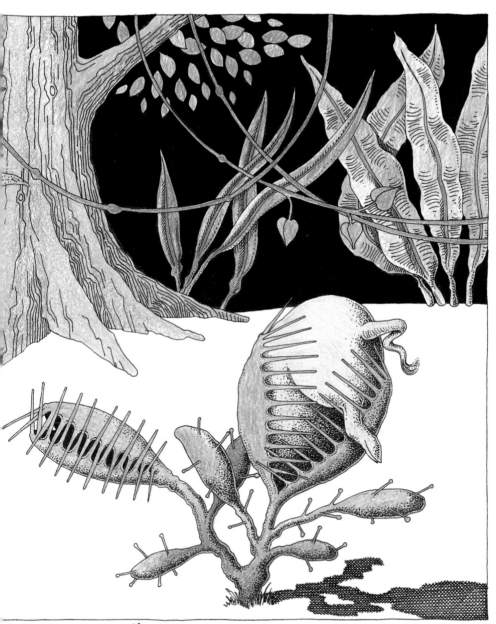

October 9ᵗʰ 1852 ; Peru :
first sighting of the Venus Pig Trap

A handsome young chap entered laughing
with a jumping bean in a jam jar;
others were balancing bottles.
It was happy hour in the swine bar.

red sty at night

Would you say I look like beef?
I'm never mistaken for lamb.
To call me veal would stretch belief.
I think and so therefore I'm ham.